SPEAKING IN TEARS

SPEAKING IN TEARS

THE POETRY IN GRIEF

GRACE ANDREN

ANCOR PRESS~PAPERBACK
KANSAS CITY

AnCor Press
An Imprint of J JAF Publishing, LLC
PO Box 46685
Kansas City, MO 64188

Speaking In Tears: The Poetry In Grief

Photographs released by Creative Commons Zero License;
Beauty girl cry by @chepko; Sad girl by @Porechenskaya;
Water drop photo by xjbxjhxm.

For information about special discounts for bulk purchases, please contact
AnCor Press/ Grace Andren at above address or at
graceandren@graceandren.com

First AnCor paperback edition 2018

Cover Design by AnCor Press
Interior Design by AnCor Press

Print ISBN: 978-1-944599-16-4
Kindle ISBN: 978-1-944599-17-1
EPub ISBN: 978-1-944599-18-8

In loving memory of my Andrea.

"Those who do not weep, do not see."
—Victor Hugo
Les Misérables

FROM GRACE

This book has been a labor of love, tears, and heartache. I'm not the only mother to have lost a child. It's not a unique position, but it's one I pray few must occupy.

It has taken me years to write the words contained within *Speaking in Tears* and while I don't profess to be a poet, they are rather poetic in style.

I began to express my pain and grief through written form at the beginning of 2014. It became my passion but in doing so, I had to move through the grieving process all over again. The pain of my loss became fresh and stabbing making it difficult to write too much at once.

These pages are filled with those words about grief and hope; pain and sorrow; and loss in its many varied forms. The pieces are about my daughter, my son, my husband, my family, and my friends. But they are also about you and yours— because grief is a universal language just like tears.

Tears span every language and country—no interpretation is needed. They speak for themselves and in a language we can all decipher. Fear, sadness, laughter, anger—our tears tell many stories.

Throughout the book you'll find that I paired my words with various black and white pictures to add to the overall experience and emotion.

My Andrea loved to pick flowers and oftentimes came back with weeds but she didn't care because they were all beautiful to her. I've included several flower pictures—for her.

Also, I want to encourage you to take a moment to tell those around you—your spouse and kids; your friends and family—whomever. Please, tell them how much you love them.

Life changes in a blink.

We can be taken off our chosen path to walk another—with no map, no choices, and no direction—lost in heart and lost in spirit.

Don't live with regrets. Don't pray for second chances. Make second chances! Don't look back on your life and say, *I wish I would have.*

I was given no choices, no ability to make a second chance. No, that option was beyond me and her. Because in that blink of an eye—all was lost and my life was irrevocably changed. My only regret is that I had so few years with her. But I treasure every single moment I was given.

I hope that my words will resonate with *you* and help *you* through whatever loss you might be grieving.

—Grace

Memories saturate my heart and
the story of you spills from my eyes.

—Grace Andren

SPEAKING IN TEARS

SPEAKING IN TEARS

As you read through the pieces complied in *Speaking in Tears*, you will notice they are dark and sad at the beginning but progress towards hope and light as you move through the book.

They are presented much like the five stages of grief described by Elisabeth Kübler-Ross.

Denial, Anger, Bargaining, Depression and Acceptance. And I would add Hope to the list after Acceptance.

These stages are very fluid. You will find yourself moving back and forth between them. Grief is not a *one-size-fits-all* process. It's very individual and the journey will be filled with peaks and valleys. Tidal pools and tsunamis. For me, grief is much like the ocean, as it will come in waves to ebb and flow like the tide.

Things might be going well and you've finally managed to catch your breath when out of the blue—a scent, a song, a child's laughter triggers a memory and you're drowning yet again.

There is no end point with grief. There won't be a time when you can say to yourself—*today, I am done with grief*. Because to be honest, that day will never come.

However, there will come a time when you're almost comfortable with the grief that you wear. At some point grief will become a part of who you are and *almost* indistinguishable from the other parts that make you—you!

Grief is by far the most profound display of love.

I think of it like this—I have hazel eyes, brownish-grey hair and grief. It's just who I am now—my new normal.

My advice for whatever you are grieving—be it a way of life, a child, a spouse, a parent, a friend, or a pet. No matter what your grief is—be gentle with yourself. The pain, the tears, and the sorrow are normal and part of the process. But give yourself permission to feel joy. It's okay to smile, to laugh, and to live.

—Grace

SOAKED

These words are soaked in pain and
strained through a grieving soul.

LITTLE PIECES

Capturing words from my heart
   like restless butterflies set free into the wind
   like releasing my soul into a great unknown
     but with no way to defend
     little pieces of who I am
     out there for all to read.

My story is right there within these lines
   my grief, my passion, my love and my needs.

Should I try to recapture the words that I speak
   as they ebb and flow within me?

No, that'd be futile
   like harnessing the wind
   like holding back the sea
     these words need to be seen
     —if only by me.

Each one gives my soul a moment of respite and
   my heart a measure of relief
   by stitching the fractures back together
     with my grieving ink.

ANDREN

MY TEARS

my voice was silent
  but my tears spoke eloquently
    each quiet drop a story of you.

HEARTACHE

Do you ever feel as if your skin and
bones are merely a container for the
pools of heartache drowning your soul?

FRAGILE

Do you ever feel as if the slightest touch
no matter how gentle would shatter your
fragile heart into a shower of tears?

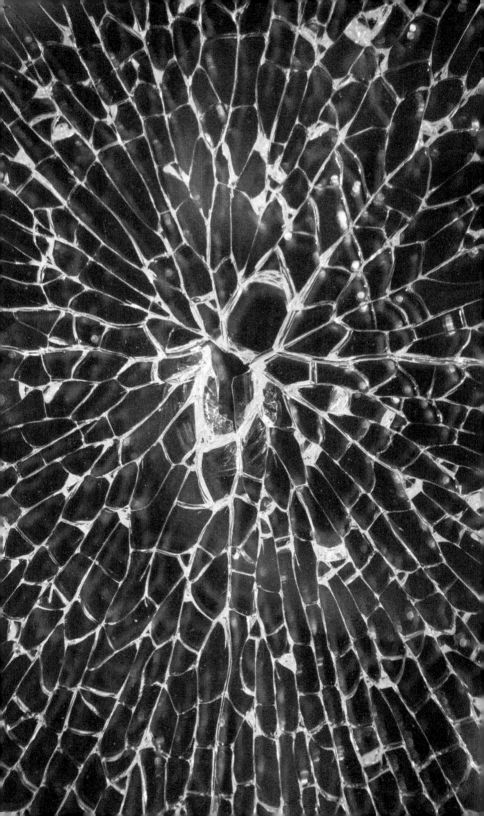

SHOULD I

Should I write our story forged in blood and
    ink the words on these pages for all to see?
Should I tell of the screams that haunt my dreams?
Should I tell of the crash that my life so thrashed?

In my mind, my heart, my soul
   I scream for you, for me, for us
      wishing we had more time together.

Not all screams are heard
   Not all wishes come true
      Not all prayers are answered.

I should know
   I've been living every day without you.

ANDREN

SCREAMING

As the date approaches,
　　the pain in my soul
　　　　encroaches upon my grieving heart
　　　　　　overwhelming it with sorrow.
How do I make through another tomorrow?

For every moment,
　　every breath is a reminder
　　　　of all that I have lost and
　　　　　　I fear at what cost.

If you're quiet and happen to listen
　　you just might hear my soul screaming—
　　　　never dreaming.

I learned to keep her muffled
　　lest the plaintive wail
　　　　rupture my heart and
　　　　　　shatter my soul apart.

WHAT IS

I wish that I could protect you from the heartache to come. I would wrap you in a bubble of what should be—

    far, far away from what is.

BEFORE AND AFTER

Why is there always a before and after? Isn't that how we speak of life in general? Before I graduated from high school and after I graduated from college. Before I was married and after I had kids. It follows this pattern through most of our lives.

But for some people there is that *ONE* defining moment by which all other events are measured and all comparison stops.

Because for those unfortunate few, there is only—
    The Before and After.

IMMUNITY

None of us are immune to deaths calling.

GRACE

34

SERIAL POETRY

The following serial poetry should be read in order, as they tell a story—one poem at a time.

The Call
Flight
Chaos Reigns
Torn
Truth
Vigilant
Bleed
Fear
Why
It's Okay
Valiant
Despair
Gone
Mend
Through Her
Dreams
Mourning
My Heart Stays

ANDREN

THE CALL

Eyes drifting shut
   too heavy to fight
Pulled under
   by the sandman's dust
In beautiful dreams
   my mind does trust
Discordant wailing
   that doesn't belong
Strident sounds
   no soothing lullaby song
A deep vibration
   a pounding felt and finally heard
Muffled sounds
   quite possibly words
Mind hazed
   soul dazed
Heart racing
   soul bracing
Grabbing the receiver
   whispering, "Hello?"
Incomprehension
   immediate tension
Stumbling to the door
   collapsing to the floor.

GRACE

ANDREN

FLIGHT

A single moment
  shallow breaths
Mind a chaotic whirl
  emotions spin and twirl
Scenes pass by
  in a frantic blur
Obstacles at every turn
  increasing steady burn
    searing every nerve
Wishing I had wings to fly
  not crawling along barely getting by
Dodging left
  then right
Straining for a glimpse—
Up above and overhead
  a bird takes flight
    disappearing into the wild
Breathless—
  all stood still.

CHAOS REIGNS

Time speeds forward
  yet stays the same
    eyes close and open again
My landscape remains unchanged
Chaos continues to reign
Sounds muffled
  then screaming loud
    words rapid-fire
      reports from a gun
One after another
  until I'm completely undone
Drowning in uncertainty
  fear permeating my every cell
Soul shivering
  forging through hell
Heart slowly unraveling
Hope bleeds
  one painful drop at a time.

TORN

A soul being torn in three—
   wishing I could replicate me
How do I possibly choose?
How could I have known which to do?
Paralyzed with indecision
   tears blur my exhausted vision
My heart pulls one way
   my soul the other
Wife
Mother
Choices, yet no choice at all
Our children
Our future
Or what should have been
A willow swaying in the changing winds
   —bending,
      so close to breaking.

ANDREN

TRUTH

Maneuvered like a puppet on strings
   towards a destiny unimagined
      an emotional devastation unfathomed
Wanting to turn off the answers
   running through my brain
In blissful ignorance
   I'd rather have lain
Where hope could be nourished
   in my ignorance it would flourish
But false hope is no hope at all
   only a delusion to blind
So in truth I will stand
   even as life pours through my fingers
      like an hourglass sifting grains of sand.

VIGILANT

Metal pulls across skin
delicate, yet brutal
praying it's not futile
Voices come from every direction
some with honesty, most with deflection
but my ears discern the difference
my eyes can clearly see the evidence
Sounds of a heartbeat fast, then slow
undecided which way to go
Uncertainty keeps me vigilant
time blurs to precious seconds.

BLEED

Another message delivered
  words that make my hands quiver
Holding tight to the receiver
  one thought to be safe
    hanging on by mere threads
      pulled from death
        time and time again
I hear the words
  but they fade and start to blend
The rug's coming out from under again
  faltering where I stand
Deep breaths
  Straighten spine
    Head up
      Knees lock
  I
    Must
      Be
        The
          Rock
No time to think
Right now, right here
  I just have to deal
    there's no time to feel
Later—
  later I'll let the emotions bleed free.

ANDREN

45

FEAR

As day turns to night
   my eyes remain wide
    too afraid to sleep
     bedside vigils I keep
Like a blood dyscrasia
   metastasizing through my soul
    fear invades my very marrow
     —anticipating sorrow
Prayers sent
   but not received
Begging
   Bargaining
    Continuing to believe.

GRACE

WHY

No hand is too small to make a difference
    yours changed the world in a single instance
Courageous—loving—selfless
    perfect words for describing you.

Courageous for how you fought
    despite the desperate odds
Loving for how your spirit shined
    embracing all that you are
Selfless for how you loved and
    cared for others before yourself.

Oh God, please!
    I begged, gently cradling her hand
My life in exchange for hers
    I'll forfeit my every breath and
      give them all to her
I thought I was exempt.

    Why, I scream?
      Why me?
        Why not, was the reply
    Indeed, why not.
But how?

    How do I let her fly?

ANDREN

IT'S OKAY

Sister and brother
   precious moments together
Pressing her little hand into clay
   remembrances to have and to display
A final bath with warm water and endless tears
   anointing my baby girl
Searching for the courage to say goodbye
Whispering brokenly—
   it's okay for you to go
     it's okay for you to fly

When my time finally comes
   I'll meet you somewhere over that rainbow
     but for now, you are part of the special ones
     too beautiful to contain within this mortal world
You, my darling have wings to unfurl
So again, I whisper softly into your little ear
   just loud enough for you and me to hear—

The sun is shining and the sky is blue
   it's okay to go
     I love you, baby girl.

VALIANT

Valiant heart and a courageous fighter
She fought hard through the long, dark night
and with a final, joyful breath
She went fearless into death.

ANDREN

DESPAIR

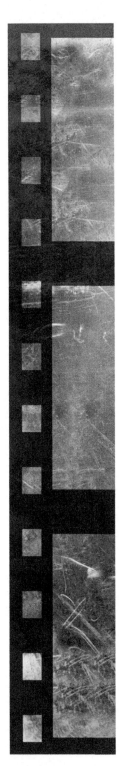

Moments captured
like a movie in review
images I keep and
treasure of you.
Some searing my mind
such painful visions
praying *those* will
eventually diminish.
Searching for answers
though none shall be found
what lesson was learned
except to forever yearn.

A week went past
we laid you to rest
drowning in grief with
no appreciable relief
Wanting to crawl in and
lay down beside you
to close my eyes and
give in to despair.
But I can't, I won't
my life remains here
whether I will it or no.

GRACE

GONE

gone
you're just gone and
I'm left with a gaping hole
where you had fit perfectly into my soul.

MEND

How am I to grow and to learn
when my eyes can't see past my tears that burn?
And my ears can't hear
over the catch in my every breath?

How do I step forward
when I'm collapsing where I stand?
How do I discover the core of who and what I am
when my world shall never spin again?
But oblivious to me,
time moves forward and at rapid speed.

Humbled at every turn
by many a stranger and my friends
I found a way for my fractured heart to mend.
Despite the heavy shadows and the rain
through your strength, I found a way to stand.

Nestled deep within my soul
I carry your boundless courage and your love
like a luminescent glow.
And while I may never again be whole
I no longer feel so broken and alone.

THROUGH HER

I try not to dwell
  on every possible what if
Pain and heartache
  will push me right over that cliff
It won't change what is and
  what became my new reality
I choose to focus on how through her
  I discovered me and a new strength set free
So I try to live by her loving example
  by opening my heart to others
Even though it often ends in failure
  I prefer to be exposed than closed
    naive over jaded
She was my role model
  my inspiration.

DREAMS

I long for those moments
   when you visit my dreams
      in glorious, vivid color and
         glowing like golden sunbeams.

Rainbow hued flowers
   below our strolling feet
      carpeting the meadow about us and
         every which way we can see.

Butterflies flying about
   dancing to and fro
      like little ballerina's
         forever on the go.

Here I can touch you
  here I can hold you
    or until dawn's pink sky comes anew
      pulling me once more
        from my beautiful dreams of you.

Quickly kissing your sweet little cheeks
  before our time comes to an end
    awakening to bittersweet tears, yet again.

Longing, always longing for the night
  but I'd cry a river of tears
    as I have through these many years
      for just one more glimpse of you.

ANDREN

MOURNING

I refused to wear black. My heart balked at the thought. Not that anyone necessarily thought that I should wear black, but there was just no way I could do it. We would be celebrating her life today—and I wouldn't have it any other way.

Besides, I didn't need dark clothes to show the world that I was grieving. It was written clear as day upon my face in the dark-purple smudges under my devastated eyes. It was there within the hollows of my pale face and with the tears that slid silently, yet endlessly down my wet cheeks, chapping the delicate skin with their ceaseless flow.

There were just too many ways to describe the grief that I wore. So, if I had worn dark clothing—I would have been rendered virtually invisible, lost to the shadows that were consuming me. Color had been a necessity—just so that I could be found amongst the living.

MY HEART STAYS

A perfect day to say goodbye
 blue skies and golden sunshine
Enormous trees to rest under
 like silent sentinels guarding over.

But those lovely rays hurt my grieving eyes
 saturated with tears, silently I cried
Doves above and you lowered below
 handfuls of dirt rain upon shiny white
 unclear how we'll make it through every night.

A sea of flowers in varying hues
 all delivered here just for you.

Fading from sight
 agony and panic take flight
Gathering every flower I can reach
 throwing them over you—
 a petaled blanket for your final sleep.

Jealous of every flower for where it lie
 wishing with you, I could have died.

Slowly turning and walking away
 but with you—
 my heart forever stays.

THE WEIGHT OF SORROW

When your emotions feel heavy enough to weigh and
your heart stutters under the weight—
how do you breathe?

HOLLOWED

Raging at the clear blue sky
How *it* dares to bathe this hollow me
   in its shimmery, golden light
I want to run and hide in mournful fright
Wanting to revel in my empty pit
   light antithesis to how dark I feel
Slowly withering, I'm dying inside

   That to my regret is what's real.

SPUN GLASS

words written
   painful extrications
   from a heart in
   mournful stasis
     —ice encases

spun glass tears
   made fragile
   through the years
   left transparent
     —paper thin.

ECHO

Silent moments within my heart echo your absence as profoundly as the quiet tears that slide endlessly down my pale hollow cheeks

DENIED

There are no words to describe
the suffocating feeling of a longing denied.

It's agony.

I long to touch her
but can't.
I long to see her
but won't.
I long to tell her so many things
but those words were abandoned upon my tongue
where they erode like acid—never to be spoken.

She won't hear all the words I would have said.

Did she hear my whispered, *I love you?*

A question with no answer—my heart weeps.

GRACE

RAGE

some days my heart is quiet
today it wants to rage

EVISCERATED

crawling over the bloody
splintered pieces of
my eviscerated soul
scraping the bits into a pile
trying to remake me whole.

BEFORE THE DAWN

I'm still here
on my knees
trying to stifle
my heart's
grieving screams.

Can you hear my souls
plaintive wails—
does it reach you there
beyond the veil?

I'm so sorry
I'm trying
to be strong
but my days seem
so endless, so very long.

I know it's darkest
before the dawn—
waiting for those
first delicate rays.

I need them
to bathe me
in golden light
helping me through
my endless night.

ANDREN

ABSENTIA

Living but not present
  my will to be—death stole
  leaving behind
  an endless mournful hole.

If I took its measure
  naming my four sided missing treasure
  Winter, Spring, Summer, Fall
  is what you'd be called.

A side for every season and filled
  with all the reasons I'm missing you.

Spring—
  When you came to me
    a magical being with butterfly wings
    shining brightly—a luminescence all could see.

Summer—
  You were too beautiful to behold
    a sweet angel you were always told
    how I loved watching you flourish and grow.

Fall—
    My breath stopped here with yours
        my life ended there with yours
        it all became a constant blur
        an abyss of longing that just won't end
        unfathomable pain with no reason to mend.

Winter—
    My constant companion
        frozen and buried alive
        slowly dying on the inside
        wanting to lay down and succumb
        to my inevitable death
        joining my heart, my soul, and
        my will at last.

It's the promise of you and what might be
    that keeps me going though on bended knee
    head bowed in supplication
    hopeful with anticipation
    praying it will come to be

United again—
    you and me.

ANDREN

PRISMS

she fell asleep clinging to wishes
dreams colored in tear-refracted light
prisms of rainbows encase her fragile heart.

BETRAYAL

when a smile feels like a betrayal to the heart.

A PALE PINK SKY

My dreams are filled with you
I relive every single memory
   the whole night through
Precious gems I hold and savor
   until dawn paints a pale pink sky and
I awaken to tears streaming and questioning—
   Why? Why am I here living without you?
Though everywhere I turn I see you there
   I hear your musical laughter
   I smell the sweet scent of your hair.
Why must I rouse to each new day
   when within those memories I wish to stay?
Every sleeping—waking cycle it begins again
   God, how I want to stay there and breathe you in.

But it's only an illusion—wishful thinking
   I have no control
For each morning you're ripped away and
   I have to watch you go.
Then each night when I close my eyes
   I welcome you into my empty arms
You willingly come back, but then you have to go—
   over and over our cycle goes
   until one day I will refuse to awaken alone.
So until then, I await each day long and for
   the moment we meet again—
   drifting along on a lullaby song.

ANDREN

TEARS

when the heart reaches emotional capacity
spilling the overflow upon your cheeks
anointing them with your pain and joy
　—evidence for all to see.

ETHEREAL

I held ethereal beauty
in the palm of my hands
setting it free with angel given wings
heart soaring and crying simultaneously.

TWENTY-ONE

the day approaches
to celebrate and reflect
heart weeps as hours pass.

RAISE A GLASS—
MAKE A TOAST

Please take a moment tonight
   Raise a glass, make a toast
For today she would have been
   21
Life to have just begun
   An adult and on her way
Instead—
   We will have to celebrate in her place
     for she is beyond hunger
      she is beyond pain and suffering
But she will never be beyond
   My memory
   My heart
   My love.

GRACE

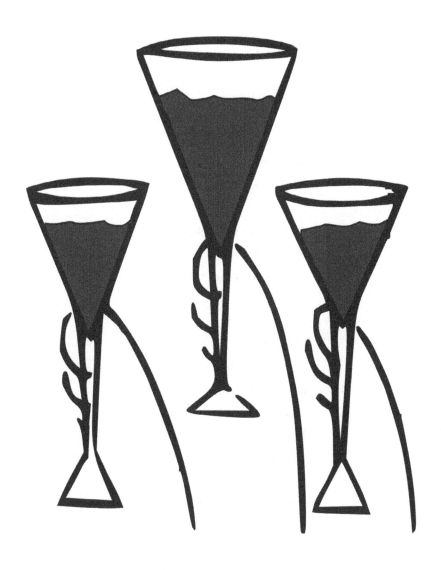

ANDREN

I SMILE

time: a dichotomous witch!

when life feels—
    simultaneously endless and
    the longing you feel
    to hold your loved one
    fair cripples your soul

yet, the loss feels so fresh
    that the tears have yet to
    dry upon your wet cheeks.

that dichotomy—
    still shreds my heart
    but I'll smile through
    every anguished tear
    that forever falls
    because that is what
    she would want me to wear

so for you, baby girl—
    I smile.

Sixteen years of missing you.

GRACE

SUNSET

Why?
Why does sunset come so early
   creeping stealthily but occurring rapidly
      denying the beauty of a life yet to live?

All becoming harsh shades of silver and grey.

How to beat back the sweeping of night
   fight the snuffing of all light?

Courage, hope, and faith
   all that's left
      for a soul bereft.

ANDREN

THIS VOID

Are you still there
   just beyond this void I feel?
Am I delusional?
Wasn't what we had truly real?
I can't imagine you leaving me here
   wandering in desolation
      all alone and full of fear.
In my need for a kindred spirit,
   a tender heart—
      did my mind make you up
        then tear it all apart?
Was I not deserving of your love?
   Were we not brought together
      by someone up above?
I'm forlorn and forsaken,
   my trust taken.
But I will continue to hold on to hope
   praying this void will Not be the end.
Despite my confusion and my pain
   you will always be my friend.

NO ESCAPE

Lost wandering inside my head
   trying to find what can't be found
   looking for a way to escape
   the many ghosts that surround.

I try to leave them at every turn
   only to find myself immersed
   in the pain and misery
   I must now relearn.

Delusional to think
   they'd ever been left behind
   for they are ever circling—
   circling my mind.

GRACE

ENDLESS NIGHT

Teetering on a precipice
   the edge of a desolate plane
So many days I've wandered
   this lonely, darkened land
A soul dying but searching—
   looking for the light
Finding a way through
   this wretched, endless night.

ANDREN

TIES THAT BIND

The ties that bind
   are anchored in the mind
   fortified by the heart
   never to be torn apart.

Those first steps taken
   when you're forced
   to your knees
   grief shaken.

No light reaches
   that inner cell
   the sad darkness
   still prevails.

Pleading for respite
   jaggedly desperate.

Praying for the dawn
   praying for the sun
   wishing this grief undone.

GRACE

COLLIDING

In my dreams I find you.
Beautiful memories.
Only to awaken—
devastated.
Dreams colliding.
Harsh reality reminding—
What is and
will never be.

DROPS OF SORROW

My eyes have wept
  like a crying sky in spring
tears rolling down my cheeks
  to drip off my chin
    in silent relief
yet, balanced on my fingertips
  each drop of sorrow
    sits and waits—
wondering where it shall land
  when I fling it to its fate.

ABSOLUTE SILENCE

Thoughts and feelings keep flitting about
   confused as whether to cry, scream or shout
Some days I just can't categorize how I feel
   can't pin down anything to clarify what is real
I crave a moment of absolute silence
   no whisperings from my racing mind
     no crying from a soul that wanted more time
Just a little respite, tired of feeling desperate
   calm—in the eye of life's chaotic storm
Maybe then my spirit could be reborn
   rejuvenated to withstand life beyond the norm
For that is where I have lived
   for too many years to count.

But this will pass, just like the last
    fortitude and gratitude, thankfully—
        go hand in hand
Giving me the ability
    to crawl my way up and eventually stand
Even when I'd been taken out at the knees
    over and over despite my whispered pleas
But I will keep searching, looking for those
    precious moments
Ones that I can call my own
    and for a brief second
        find solace in my momentary peace.

EXSANGUINATING

smiling
laughing
   an expert at hiding
      all the pain that resides
      bleeding inside
   exsanguinating
      one drop of sorrow at a time
      my soul forever red.

TURBULENT

Hiding from life
   endless strife
Drowning under the waves
   no need to be brave
Soul searching
   seeking the light
Suffocating darkness
   heart staining blight
Cleansing—all that remains
   to rid me of residual blame
My spirit refuses, still fighting me
   thus remaining as turbulent as the sea.

PENNED

I fell asleep reading your letters again
those words your heart had penned
I keep them tied in a bundle at my bedside
each one neatly etched on my insides.

Shall I recite each verse written for me
those whispered words offer no relief
my heart and soul cry in disbelief.

Tears soak through the pages and
smear the ink—destroying my only link
to you and the love we shared our life through.

SKIMMING

Surveying my emotions
looking for something to find
but apparently nothing
is occupying my mind

Am I numb?

In shock?

Skimming along
in a state of disbelief
perhaps—I don't really know
it's like I'm a blank canvas
with no colors to show.

SHADOW

shadow of a girl
seeking the light
afraid to step
beyond the night
searching the stars
sprinkled dust.

BREATH HELD

when goodbye feels but a breath away.

COALESCE

Days when I want to ignore what
   my mind astutely has to say
say what my heart screams
   at deaf ears most days.

Warring emotions of heart and mind
   with each side scoring
scoring my soul to bleeding
   with their abject warring.

Coalesce divergent factions
   with the intent to possess
possess the fortitude needed
   for my heart, mind, and soul
      to coalesce.

*Written as a Mirror Sestet

BASKING

A lonely road
   mired in heartache
longing to feel the sun
   through the trees.

The clouds are breaking
   if only for a moment and
I'm basking within
   that one lonely ray of sunshine.

FADING AWAY

Weary from endless blinding days
   colors are leached to simple shades of grey
      constantly bleeding, forever fading away
Reaching for memories harbored deep within my soul
   beautiful vignettes glowing in delicate rainbow hues
      I'll color my heart with those
         indelible shades of you.

ANDREN

MEMORY LANE

A trip down memory lane
   a path overflowing with pain
The ground beneath my feet
   remains saturated with tears
   even after all these years
Along this path that I now walk
   I search for the happy memories and
   the sad—so that we might have a talk
There are so many things I need to say
   but as my words make their way
   from heart to lips
   grief closes my throat
   making it a short trip
Choking on every syllable
   I wanted to you to hear
   my tears will have to do
   for every single one
   was shed for you.

OBLIVION

At the edge of oblivion
where decisions are made
where the sea will rage
with a ferocity mirroring
the turmoil within a soul torn
bleeding and raw
struggling with whether
to embrace the light
or let it fade
darkness pulls
whispering of sweet release
a respite
if for only one breath
one heartbeat of silence.

ANDREN

CREEPING SHADOWS

Mind screaming havoc
  thoughts that slay
Like bumblebees stinging
  at whatever they may
Some things should
  just be left alone
But these are itching
  for the damned light of day
    so they can swallow me whole
    taking away this new found home
But the ground is made of
  remorse and thorns and
    creeping shadows that roam
    enveloping all my hope.

So I'm digging deep and digging in
   holding off these thoughts
   clawing at me to win
Determined to rip my heart
   to pieces and parts
I submit to the inevitable
   for I am no longer capable
      to fight this rising tide
      of what's lying in wait
      for what resides
   a mere breath away
      —waiting.

WINTERSCAPE

Winterscape heart
  desolate days
frozen layers
  keeping spring at bay
endless searching
  hoping to find the way
  to my lost soul.

SHARDS OF GLASS

Here before—
   watching you go
tears wet my cheeks
   like lost words
     a strangled voice
each drop
   fragments from my heart
     conveying what I could not
the evidence without
   conveys nothing
     of what's contained within
like a thousand shards of glass
   ripping through my soul
     suffocating me
      with their unabated flow
your fallout has come
   haunting my every tomorrow.

GRACE

THOSE

those moments when your heart
    can't decide what to feel
those nights—alone
    when aching to love
softly whispered litany
    soulful cry echoing.

SPOOL OF HOPE

Benign words strung together have the capacity
to unravel the stoic of souls and mine feels like
an empty spool of hope wound around
a fragile soul of dreams.

WHEN

When you're drowning
   on an ache that overwhelms

When the tears come so fast and heavy
   that you can't breathe

When you're dropping to your knees
   regardless of the pain

When you want to scream
   for the unjust and unfair things

When you just don't want
   to take another breath
      because the pain of each inhalation
      feels like a knife driven home
         eviscerating you to the bone
         until your gutted
            your life forever rutted
      dejected, rejected

—Lost and alone.

ANDREN

123

DROWN

I wish I could drown in numbness
allowing the current to pull me under the waves
where all is quiet and I can hear the weeping of
my soul.

OCEANS

lost in an ocean of grief
    fingers cling to the cutting reef
the tide is high
    but I am low
      struggling through the waves
      trapped in the undertow.

PER*M*ISSION

crying for others
when you can't cry for yourself.

ANDREN

HIDDEN

I thought of you today
which isn't unusual to say.

Conversing with a friend
I spoke of where I'd been
how far I've come and
how much I missed you still.
when suddenly tears wet my eyes
against my will.

As I continued to tell my friend
about you and of all the things
I planned to do, I had to force the sobs
to remain hidden—
not wanting to share that part of my pain
that part of me.

But with each breath I attempted to use
stifling what tried to escape,
the harder each consecutive breath was to
take
I was in a panic not to reveal
all that I still feel.

How sometimes I drown and
can't find my way 'round
but I finally managed each painful word said,
though with a broken whisper
past my lips they had bled.

ANDREN

129

FRAGMENTS

Why is it I can bear
my tears and my pain
but not yours?
No, yours will gut me and
eviscerate my soul
into glittering pieces
—fragments of what was once whole.

CENTURIES

How can it feel as if a century has come and gone?
A hundred years of an endless winter season
my heart lays fallow waiting upon the spring.

PATCHED

Lovely and bright
   joyful and forthright
      always a kind word and a smile
Her presence a soothing balm
   to those who would know her
      but no one truly did
For underneath that smile she hid
   the pain that she was truly in
Never wanting to be a burden
   she patched her soul on her own
Carefully placed bandages— worn thin
      blood and pain seeping through
      her smile just a little blue
But like a ballerina dressing for center stage
   her pointe shoes concealed
      what she was unable to reveal
A diversion from the pain
   her smile hides the same.

ANDREN

133

LUNAR

Whether a full moon or
   a new moon
every lunar cycle
   sees my empty arms
reaching for you—
   my love,
     so far away.

ANEMIC

For years we subsisted
   in the shadows of the moon
our world grievingly anemic
   devoid of vibrant colors
for the sun had departed with you.

QUIESCENCE

If the words were rendered into print
   brought to life upon this page—
   would their impart be immediate?
Or shall I have time to mourn,
   to grieve their significance?
Will there be quiescence for my heart first,
   to prepare for the devastation?
For the deluge,
   the drowning of my soul?

PRESSED AND SAVED

A journal of sorts
sorrow written
pages rarely seen
Kept tucked away
roses from that day
pressed and saved
Visited upon occasion
when I need the pain
the reminder
of what had been
The visceral reaction
keeps me sane
keeps me grounded
in the undeniable truth
Life is too short not to live
—so live it.

ANDREN

SOUND OF SILENCE

At times I am comfortable within
the silence that comes between,
at times though, it's loud enough
to be heard as deafening screams.

Layers and bricks keep building up and
I feel their rough texture
each and every time I reach out
to touch you with my hesitant fingers.

How do I scale that which I did not build?
How do I find my way through these darkest fields?

I know not what to do
as my heart is broken and bleeding you
haunted and hollowed,
lost wandering about and reaching.

Oh, how I'm reaching
for that which I can not see.
it's there—just there
beyond my heart's screaming,
or maybe it's just lost to me now
lost to the dreaming.

GRACE

CRYSTALLINE

everyday I pray
    for my pain to be dead
of winter landscapes
    desolate but unafraid
too many crystalline teardrops
    I have bled.

CHAOTIC

Chaotic and swirling
emotions twirling
tumbling in my abyss
searching for why I exist.

Where are the answers I seek?
I've been plumbing, looking deep.

Someone, please take my hand
show me where I am
help me find the way past
the dark drowning today.

MERCY

Words echoing from the past
   take me unawares
they haunt and they chill
   forcing me to kneel
   onto knees that bleed
my shattered heart pleads
   for mercy once more.

SHATTERED

I've touched that bruise too much as of late
—remembering
now it bleeds uncontrollably and
my heart weeps in time and
my soul is hollow
—yet again.

SORROW

Hearts are meant to beat a soft lub-dub
    lulling you to sleep but—
all I hear is a plaintive wailing
all I hear is my heart failing
    drowning in sorrow.

SWIFT

joy,
    so foreign an emotion
    barely surviving
    life's simple motions

first smiles and
    first laughs

crying with
    every single breath

guilt swift
    to settle deep

pain and sorrow
    never sleep.

SUNSET COMES

Each stuttering heartbeat a reminder that every breath is precious and the magnificent colors glowing within the sunset will touch us all eventually.

Rest not among the idle for all souls
will have their final slumber.
Seek each new dawn and chase every sunset.
Live complete unto your last breath replete.

A GENTLE BREEZE

Eyes closed and face tilted to the sun, a
gentle breeze tickles my lashes and stirs
my hair. My heart reminisces at the
beautiful memories housed and sheltered
there. I visit them as often as I can but
sometimes it's more than I can bear.

REACHING

I'm looking forward
  but falling back
drowning under
  the weight again
my path—
  it's not yours
it's meandering slowly,
  so slowly but moving
reaching for hope
  it's fragile, yet resilient
barriers drop and break
  light shines through open cracks
my soul worn paper thin
  allowed hope and love
    to slide right in.

ANDREN

TRAVELING

A soul traveling through time
   dimensions out of line
searching endlessly
   limping along listlessly
awake, but in automation
   praying for spiritual animation
seeking worthy purpose
   roots gripping for solid purchase
releasing those invisible chains
   for they constrict and they maim
veils lifting from blind eyes
   truly seeing for the first time
hope amongst the ruins and strife
   heart renewed to stuttering life.

lost in a vortex of pain
where only
darkness reigns
my naked
grieving soul
is exposed
lost and confused
trying to find
my way home
back to you.

GRACE

———

PETALS

Each word cried upon my page
    tears of love, grief and silent rage
       like petals plucked from a flower
       in a waterfall—
         a petaled shower
     accompanied by the silent refrain
        Love me and love me not
life given and life taken
     my soul left shaken
for each petal reveals more of me
     till one day I'll be just a stem
        —barren
hoping I might have petals again
     just to shed them anew
       sharing all that I am
        with you.

ANDREN

BLUSHING

she sheds her light upon us
every day, but today
she awakened a bit shy,
blushing pretty in pink
hopes for a new day.

LIKE MAGIC

she sheds her past
  like fall leaves
sets fire to her spirit and
  like magic
she's now free
  spring comes
to the waiting home
  of her heart.

GHOSTING

There's a road inside my heart
only you can travel there
ghosting along the trail of tears
in a whisper only I can hear
you sing to my soul.

FALTERS

when I think of writing about you
my breath falters and my heart stops.

how can I capture you on paper
when I can't see the words through my tears?

RIVER

love and remorse
   happiness and grief
     try their damnedest
      to tear me apart
I close my eyes and
    float atop my river of tears
     absorbing the memory
      of each drop shed.

WITH EACH

with each breath I take
   I embrace that I'm alive
with each beat of my heart
   I celebrate the hope that it sings
with each life I touch in kindness
   I pray that it will be passed along in full measure
with each sunset I witness
   I realize how short life has become
so...
live your life
   with love bursting from your heart
live your life
   thoughtful of what you say
live your life
   knowing today may be your last

and think to yourself—
   how would I want to be remembered
     as I take my final breath.

     —drifting in thoughtful contemplation.

MULLIONED

Eyes closed—
I envision a mullioned window to my soul
    a small opening only I can control
    allowing a bit of light to refract through
    and go wherever I send it
For healing and a helping hand
    just a little part of who and what I am
    bathing those chosen—in light and in love
I see it so clearly in my heart and in my mind
    the helping of others from time to time.

ANDREN

BUOYANT

I read your words
   the pain a visible stain
If only I could reach back
   through the years to wipe
   away your beautiful tears—
Give you a comforting hug
   filled with understanding and love
Little did you know that all this while
   you'd been nestled within the home of her soul
   buoyant on her strength and her love.

GRACE

WHISPERING

I feel you whispering
across my heart today
reminding me that
you're still there
holding my fractured pieces
lovingly in your little hands.

—missing you baby girl.

WILD AND FREE

Oh, to be free
like the wildflower
to bask in surrender
under the wide open
forgiving sky.

METAMORPHOSIS

Things are better beneath
　　hiding in the recess
　　yet, they'll surface
　　　despite our control.

Clinging to a reality that's false
　　hoping to deny
　　the laborious cross
　　　the pain we bear
　　　we can not share.

Winds of change
　　denying what they bring
　　hiding frightened in shadows
　　　refusing to begin again.

Blind to the light that shines
　　run, hide—or fly with the winds
　　buoyant on whispered fragile promises
　　　a metamorphosis begins.

GRACE

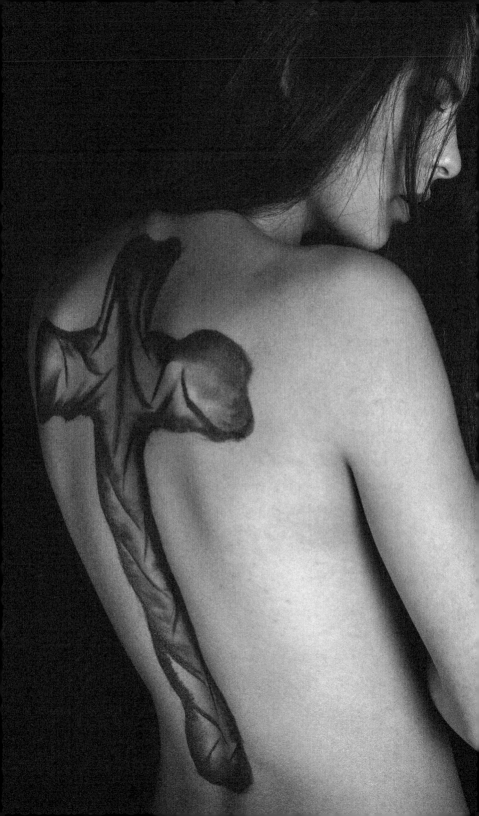

INDELIBLY ME

The reflection I see like it or not it's me.
Blonde hair turned brown and highlighted with
age though she wouldn't say that makes her
sage.

Today the mirror was not kind to me. Dark
circles and wrinkles embrace my hazel eyes—
smudged underneath with a fatigue bruised
hue, covering the evidence of illness is all this
reflection can do.

But in the mournful depths, a spark still lies. I
refuse to let go of that innocent wonder though
my heart has been repeatedly plundered. I will
continue to give, though I may not receive. I
can't change the colors that are indelibly me.

GRACE

If there's a way to give my heart and then take it back that's a skill and knowledge I currently lack. But I will not seek this type of edification. I can't live a life of stifled reservation. I choose to be joyful and giving even if my heart invariably needs mending.

We'll make it through—me and this reflection I see. We've traveled worse roads. There have been mountains and valleys—we've traversed many along the way but we've made it here and we have come so far. So with her hand in mine—I've decided we'll be just fine.

ANDREN

—

HOPE INFUSES

with each sunset that I see
  I bring to it the heavy burden of grief
but with each sunrise that follows
  hope infuses my every empty hollow.

BREATHE

Breathe through endless tears
when pain and grief
overwhelms—
laugh
to spite darkness.

HOPE BLOSSOMS

autumn sun filters softly
    through red and yellow leaves
standing within
    those glowing rays
I bathed in the light
    of new possibilities
        hope blossoming.

ANDREN

UNFETTERED

within dreams all may be found
  a shattered heart—
    whole and newly bound
      finally able to beat unfettered and free.

LOVING RESONANCE

Unable to articulate her words
music became her voice
Listen carefully and
you can hear her heart
echo through each note
Like delicate butterflies
drifting from flower to flower
A trail of pollen motes
floating along behind
Shimmering evidence of
her loving resonance.

TRAJECTORY

Life's trajectory
    fate's whimsy
Lost in a storm,
    not of my choosing
Which way is home,
    my will I'm losing
The winds of change
    dictating who I am

    Choices

Capture the wind and fly
    succumb to depression and die

Embracing this new peaceful me
    allowing my spirit to simply soar free.

DIAPHANOUS

When your smile feels as fragile as
the diaphanous wings of a delicate butterfly
just stretching for the first flight of her life.

TRANSLUCENT

as time passes
   the moments haunting my heart and
   ripping my soul apart
     are fading like pale ink upon memory's page
     —translucent.

SPRING AGAIN

Alone in my room
   silence surrounds me
   in comfort and distress
   until a warm spring shower
   moved through making life
   a little less dower.

The soft melody
   each drop played
   like tinkling bells
   pulled me to my feet
   to run outside
   on this mournful day.

Dancing, embracing,
  chasing away the pain
  with the purity of each
  beautiful drop of cleansing rain.

My heart sang
  my feet rejoiced
  my soul had a choice
  to move from winter
  to spring again

PROTECT

each petal was created with a purpose
    to protect her heart
so that her dormant soul could flower
    safe within their sheltering embrace.

FULL MEASURE

Age had weathered her eyes
   Laugh lines
   Worry lines
   Grief lines
Each one a badge
Her life lived in full measure
   A heart full of treasures.

SHADES OF GREY

As my night awakens to day
   a gentle light illuminates my grieving heart and
the oppressive darkness slowly fades
   turning to beautiful shades of grey.

ANDREN

REFLECTING

the innocent wonder that fills your soul
   I'd die to keep those colors reflecting in you and
   safe from fading.

SHINE

Can eye color change so profoundly?
Now I can wear mine so proudly
for I swear God gave me yours.

So when I look into the mirror
—there you will be staring back at me.

If only mine would shine with your inner light.
A loving soul—so beautiful and bright
immolating your courageous spirit
will be my forever mission.

You are the benchmark I hope to achieve
I only have to close our eyes,
touch your shining soul, and believe.

ANDREN

FOREVER

Time—
Distance
   this life or the next
I will always be your mother
   can't take that back
Whether breathing or not
   I am forever your adoring mom
You will always be
   my beautiful children
I will love you
   even when I'm gone and mere dust
   floating on the gentle winds
Our souls will always be united
   our love shall endure
No matter the time or distance.

GRIEF

In times of tragedy
   in times of sorrow
Lend your arms
   for a place to burrow
Lend you ears
   to listen and hear
Just be there
   be near

There are no words to mend
   the broken hearted
Especially for those
   with newly departed
Ministry of presence says more
   than words ever could

Come hold my hand
   we'll take a stand
We'll share the grief
   praying the pain will be brief
Though we know it will last
   my hand will always hold fast.

GRACE

EPIPHANY

Some epiphanies take a lifetime to form
moving slowly but inextricably from darkness
to twilight to full-blown sun

While others take you unawares like a sudden
spotlight you find yourself standing in
where all that was once hidden by shadows
is revealed with an unassailable clarity

Embrace enlightenment, allow your soul
to ascend to a higher plane.

ANDREN

BELIEVE

As the night fades to day
   awakening to fresh possibilities
as my beautiful dreams fade
   transitioning to reality
as I cling to one and
   embrace the other
as I try to find the balance
   in dreaming, longing and living
I realize even with my eyes wide open
   even with my mind and my soul coping
my heart will remain forever broken
   reality a mere token to my dreams
where you live and greet me each night
   I only have to open my mind and believe.

ALWAYS

Joy fills my soul
   like effervescent bubbles
     of liquid sunshine
Each glorious one
   floats along, keeping time
     beat for beat with my happy heart
Knowing you are always with me
   not some distant heaven apart.

ENDLESSLY

Videos of soldiers coming home
   surprising their loved ones
   they've been all alone—waiting
Can't stop the tears from flowing
   their love and happiness glowing
God, how my heart aches for just that
   how I wish I could see you once again
   to have you alive and running at me
I can only imagine how that would be
   your little arms around my neck
   tears flowing unchecked
Someday, please, let that be true
   I'd give anything, truly anything to hold you
One minute in time, sixty little seconds
   long enough to tell you how proud I am
How much I love you and how I miss you
   endlessly and every day
   —from beginning to end.

ANDREN

DAWN

Let's seek the dawn
let her chase the shadows away
there on the shores of a new day
we'll be renewed and free.

TIME

as a child
I thought I had
all the time in the world
now time slips through my fingers
fading like the final rays of sunset.

SYMPHONY

Music—
with my ears I hear
with my soul I listen
Orchestral movements
scored upon my heart
each note a memory
happy and sad
A symphony of my life.

ANDREN

209

MARKING TIME

Holding your hand
  as you hold mine
tears streak our cheeks
  each one marking time
slowly moving forward
  seeking the peace we hope to find.

And at the crossroads of hope
  we'll walk forward in grace
living every day in their place
  allowing time to bring us peace.

TODAY

Today,
    I took my first deep breath
        sweet air rushed in filling my chest
        the pain lifted just enough to breathe.

SHELTER

Held deep within my soul
   I shelter a little girl
She has wide, innocent eyes and
   I will protect her with my life
   from the heartache and the strife
   from the turmoil of this great, chaotic world
So there within my soul she'll be—
   where she lies happy, innocent and free.

ANDREN

HEALING

At the tips of my fingers
  I can feel that healing grace
I just have to stretch
  beyond my minds dark place
walking with a determined stride
  I will reach the other side.

COURAGEOUS HEART

It's the quiet strength that resonated
through her gentle soul that I carry still
her courage became my will.

MY EVERY BREATH

I would choose a lifetime of heartache and grief
over not having the chance to love you
with my every breath.

—I will miss and love you always.

I FEEL YOU NEAR

Today, I especially feel you near
   reaching for me
   through these long lonely years
I'm blessed to have two angels now
   watching over me from above
Every day I feel their encompassing love
   but at night, when lonely
   I search the stars floating by
   wondering where they are
   where they could be
   when all along they were here—
    right here with me
Right within my blind reach
   my heart only had to teach
   my mind what to see.

GRACE

I wasn't sure if I could truly believe
   but it was just like you had said
You've held my hand every day through
   pouring your love and your strength
   into a heart dying—for want of you
But our love
   —our unbreakable bond
   was strengthened even more
   by the addition of my beautiful angel new.

ANDREN

HOPEFUL

Like a newly sprouted daffodil
I too, seek the sun
Let her shine upon my upturned face
awakening to the hope of a new day.

ANDREN

PUNCH IN

Punch in
　　punch out
That's what life
　　tends to be about
Measuring moments
　　by the sweep of the hand
We can't speed it up
　　nor slow it down
It marches on despite
　　how we frown
We can't go forward
　　we can't go back
Even when we beg and
　　plead for another crack
But that moment
　　has since passed us by
All we can do
　　is watch time fly
And pray that we've learned
　　from our mistakes
And spend what time we have wise.

KEEPING TIME

Lost—confusion sets in
   never shall I walk that way again.
Perhaps if I follow the usual path set forth
   I'll find my way and fix my fractured worth.
But the road before me
   is a long and meandering one.
Endless lonely miles stretch ahead and
   I've only just begun.
Two steps forward and
   one stumbling back.
Searching for the courage
   I seemingly lack.
How do I survive these days
   all alone.
You were my life
   all I'd ever known.

Lost—within my fractured soul
   I search for where our immortal love still
   glows and drink deep from that well.
From where your endless love
   continues to dwell.
Wrapping myself
   in a tattered cloak of endless pride.
My head's held high and
   I continue on with life's wild ride.
Grieving shoulders pulled back
   my gaze lifted to the horizon.
Sighing in peace
   I feel you right next to me.
A comforting shadow
   walking along keeping time.

ANDREN

MY MAGICAL WORLD

Step into the magical world
  inside my mind.
The one in which I escape to
  all of the time.
Shedding my grief
  like a second skin in its wake.
Here I can do and be what I want
  there are no mistakes.
A graceful ballerina floating
  like a butterfly across center stage.
A character I have created and penned
  upon many a page.
A cellist playing a haunting melody
  plucked from my heart.
Notes weaving a tapestry
  born from a soul ripped apart.
A muted voice that shall finally be heard
  if only for a few precious whispered words.
To live as an actor upon life's open stage
  venting all my grief and my pent up rage.

GRACE

There's no judging
  as to what's said or done.
Here I can be carefree,
  happy and fun.
There's no sadness weighing down
  my old weary soul.
This is where I escape
  this is where I go.
When I need a reprieve
  a way to relieve the clawing ache
  that still saturates.
For this magical world of mine
  keeps me sane.
Shelters me from the tears
  drenching my heart like rain.
So step inside
  save your heart for your soul's sake.
Peace is at hand
  don't wait.
Create your own magical world
  in which you can escape.

ANDREN

FREE

My life plans are not what they used to be
  I need to set my yesterday's free
Somewhere along the way
  I lost who I was and what I had to say
I'm empty, those ideas are gone
  she died, only to be reborn
So, goodbye to who I was and will never be
  she is gone and I am free!

ALL CLEAR

sunshine follows rain
—in nature
    so too in life
hold onto hope and
   the courage to love
for when the storms pass
   eyes clear to all that's dear.

SEASONS OF FRIENDS

Friendships come and go
   like seasons in our lives.
Many cycle through over the years
   breezing by on gusty winds,
   only to dry our falling tears.

Will you only be around
   when things are lush and green?
With abundant gifts dropping ripe
   from vine and tree?
Will you fall to your knees
   plucking and harvesting all that could be?

Or will you leave some for the vine
    so that it may ripen and mature with time?
Will you weather all the storms,
    the plagues, and the imperfections of form?

Or will you come and stay
    finding all the ways
    to be everything that's needed?
Helping fallowed fields
    to be reseeded?

Lucky are the chosen few
    who have friends walking beside them
    their whole lives through.

CHRYSALIS

sightless
   flightless
      fighting my way out of the dark
awakening
   day breaking
      butterfly wings unfolding
my first taste of sunshine
   my first gentle breeze
      —delicate wings
   I'm finally free.

GRACE

CUSP

Your swirling colors of hope
beckon my soul to rise and shine
my heart on the cusp of a new day.

ANDREN

THANK YOU

I wanted to thank you for taking the time to read *Speaking In Tears*. The story of Andrea needs to be shared and this book is only the beginning, but I had to start somewhere.

I have additional poetry books planned but I'm also writing a book that will be based on a true story—her story. Her book will be written as fiction to protect the various identities contained within.

The sorrow at losing my daughter at the tender age of 5 was truly unbearable. But writing about the pain and sharing my grief has helped my husband and our family. My hope is that it will help others who are also grieving.

Thank you,
Grace

ABOUT GRACE ANDREN

For the past 19 years, Grace Andren has mourned the death of her young daughter, Andrea. It was only through her passion for writing poetry that she was able to express her grief—opening a floodgate of emotions. Joy. Sorrow. Anger. Love.

Her poetic journey through the grieving process is contained within her book, Speaking In Tears. Through her words, and their black and white photographic representation, she takes the reader from sorrow to hope.

"But moving forward is not letting go because we take our loved ones with us."

—Grace Andren

———

Let Grace know you enjoyed her book
by visiting this Hello link.
www.graceandren.com/reader-hello

Writing is fairly solitary.
So give it a visit and it will let Grace know
you're out there and reading her words.

———

Visit the author's website: www.graceandren.com

———

Be sure to "follow" Grace through her
Amazon.com author page
to be notified of her latest work.

———

Send Grace an email to be notified of New Releases
Email: graceandren@graceandren.com

GRACE

242

SPEAKING IN TEARS

ANDREN

GRACE

ANDREN

MV ANDREA

GRACE

248

ANDREN

249

GRACE

250

Made in the USA
Middletown, DE
29 March 2021